IMAGES *of* MARILYN
MONROE

IMAGES *of* MARILYN
MONROE

Edited by
Gareth Thomas

Bath · New York · Singapore · Hong Kong · Cologne · Delhi · Melbourne

First published by Parragon in 2008.

Parragon
Queen Street House
4 Queen Street
Bath, BA1 IHE

For photograph copyrights see page 224
Text © Parragon Books Ltd 2008
Cover Images © Getty Images
Back flap Image © Corbis

Produced by Atlantic Publishing

A catalogue record for this book is available
from the British Library.

ISBN 978–1–4075–1131–3
Printed in Indonesia

INTRODUCTION

In a life which was cut tragically short at the age of just 36, Marilyn Monroe managed to establish herself as a cinematic legend and icon of the twentieth century. She first made a name for herself as a model, before moving into film, where she frequently played the role of the attractive 'dumb blonde', but as an intelligent, talented and complex woman, it was a stereotype from which she would spend much of her life attempting to escape. She was also haunted by the spectre of an unsettled childhood, which appeared to translate into restlessness throughout her life, and a series of failed marriages and pregnancies did nothing to shake off her insecurities. It seems that all Marilyn Monroe really wanted was to be loved and respected and, whilst at times she may have struggled to achieve those aims during her lifetime, today, almost half a century after her death, she is almost universally adored, not just for her striking beauty, but for her wit, intellect and artistry.

Marilyn was born Norma Jeane Mortenson on 1 June 1926, in Los Angeles General Hospital and, although her father was most likely to have been Charles Stanley Gifford, a foreman at Consolidated Film Industries, where her mother Gladys worked as a film cutter, she was registered with the surname Mortenson after Gladys's second husband, Martin Edward Mortenson. However, this relationship had ended well before Norma Jeane's birth and, despite various rumours, she would never know her father's true identity.

Unmarried, and with no help from her family, Gladys struggled to make ends meet, and so Norma Jeane was soon taken in by the Bolender family, who were experienced foster carers and neighbours of Gladys's parents. In later life, Marilyn would recall her years with the Bolenders as desperately impoverished, but in fact they were able to support her comfortably, and she remained with them until the age of seven, whilst still receiving regular visits from her mother.

Then in 1933, after the traumatic death of her pet dog Tippy at the hands of a neighbour, Norma Jeane was collected by her mother, and they moved into a small Hollywood house; part of which Gladys rented out in order to pay the mortgage. The following year however, Gladys descended into depression and was committed to a psychiatric hospital, leaving Norma Jeane in the care of her friend Grace. Grace doted on Norma Jeane, but was married soon after taking her on, and so at the age of nine, Norma Jeane was placed in an orphanage. She was then briefly fostered, before returning to live with Grace and her husband Erwin Goddard.

In 1942 Erwin secured employment on the East coast, and facing a return to the orphanage, the 16-year-old Norma Jeane found a way out by marrying her 21-year-old neighbour, James Dougherty. Shortly afterwards, she found employment in a munitions factory, and it was here that she was spotted by army photographer David Conover, who suggested she might pursue a modelling career. Norma Jeane took his advice and signed up with a modelling agency, at which time she also began to bleach her hair and attend charm classes. By now, her husband had been posted overseas and, as she was able to support herself by modelling, she became increasingly independent. So much so in fact that, within four years, the marriage would be over.

Right: An early picture of Norma Jeane sitting on the running board of the Model T Ford of her foster parents, the Bolenders.

Opposite: At the beginning of her film career, the studios' publicity pictures often portrayed Marilyn as the 'girl next door' rather than the 'blonde bombshell'.

While modelling, Norma Jeane had registered with the National Concert Artists Corporation and, in the summer of 1946, she had her first screen test, on the strength of which, 20th Century Fox decided to sign her up for six months, before extending her contract to a year. Once signed, Norma Jeane adopted her stage name, and would forever be known as Marilyn Monroe.

In her year at Fox, Marilyn made appearances in just three B-movies before returning to modelling but, in 1948, she was taken up by Columbia Studios, and was given her first chance to sing, as a chorus girl in *Ladies of the Chorus*. Despite favourable notices, Marilyn's contract was not renewed but, whilst at Columbia, she had made an important ally in Natasha Lytess, who would later become

Above: Marilyn has dinner with her second husband Joe DiMaggio. The marriage was short-lived, Marilyn filing for divorce after only nine months.

Opposite: Marilyn takes direction from Billy Wilder on the set of *The Seven Year Itch*.

her personal acting coach. Another fortunate encounter followed in 1949, when Marilyn met Hollywood agent Johnny Hyde, who decided to take her under his wing. Still modelling, it was also in 1949 that Marilyn posed for some nude calendar shots, which would resurface later in her career.

The following year, with Hyde's support, Marilyn's career began to take off, and she was to appear in five films, including the high-profile John Huston movie, *The Asphalt Jungle*, and the Oscar-winning *All About Eve*. Sadly, Johnny Hyde died at the end of the year but, with his help, Marilyn had by now secured a long-term contract with Fox.

In 1951, she appeared in several small roles but, perhaps most importantly, she was given her first serious dramatic part, in Fritz Lang's *Clash by Night*, which led to her playing her first lead, in 1952's *Don't Bother to Knock*. Marilyn's popularity was then boosted by a part in the comedy *Monkey Business*, which starred Cary Grant and Ginger Rogers. However, during filming, a potential scandal loomed when it was revealed that Marilyn was the anonymous nude in a calendar published that year. Fortunately, her fans were sympathetic, and her career remained intact. Just days after the story appeared in the press, more good luck followed, when Marilyn was introduced to baseball legend Joe DiMaggio, and a romance quickly blossomed between them.

In 1953, Marilyn established her talent with a starring role in *Niagara*, before literally cementing her fame alongside Jane Russell, when they were both asked to make their mark on the pavement of Hollywood Boulevard, having starred together in *Gentlemen Prefer Blondes*. Marilyn was now becoming a box-office attraction but, after completing two further films, *How to Marry a Millionaire* and *River of No Return* in quick succession, she was beginning to find her schedule too demanding. As a result, and with the support of agent Charles Feldman, she failed to report for work on *The Girl in Pink Tights*, and was immediately suspended. However, on 14 January 1954, Marilyn and Joe DiMaggio were married in San Francisco, and the massive publicity this generated prompted Fox to reconsider their decision.

Meanwhile, Marilyn and Joe travelled to Japan for their honeymoon, where Joe was to open the 1954 baseball season, but he was dismayed when Marilyn accepted an invitation to embark on a tour of Korea to entertain U.S. troops. Joe was quite possessive and resented Marilyn's courting of male attention, which unfortunately did not bode well for their fledgling marriage.

Back in the U.S., Marilyn returned to work, whilst Feldman continued to fight her corner for an improved contract. She began filming *There's No Business Like Show Business* in May, but was still recovering from a bout of illness that she had suffered in Japan, and struggled somewhat during shooting. Additionally, it seemed that her anxieties grew in direct proportion to her workload and fame, as did her intake of prescription drugs.

Above: Marilyn and Arthur Miller pictured shortly before their wedding in the summer of 1956.

Opposite: In July 1956 the newly-married Millers left for London where Marilyn was to begin filming *The Sleeping Prince* with Laurence Olivier and Arthur Miller planned to work on a production of his play *A View from the Bridge*.

Almost immediately after completing the movie, Marilyn was off to New York to begin work on *The Seven Year Itch*. The film was a massive success, and not only proved that Marilyn was a talented comedic actress, but contained one of the most iconic moments in the history of the cinema; when her skirt is lifted by the wind as she stands on a subway grating. However, having attended the filming of the sidewalk scene, Joe DiMaggio was enraged to see his wife showing her underwear being cheered by the crowds, and this was almost the final straw for their already flagging marriage. By October, Marilyn announced that they were to divorce.

Marilyn's relationship with 20th Century Fox was also under strain at this time, and so, seeking greater artistic freedom, she relocated to New York at the end of 1954, where she was to announce the formation of her own company, Marilyn Monroe Productions, in association with the photographer, Milton Greene.

During her time in New York, Marilyn was also to forge some important new relationships. She began attending the Actors Studio, where she received training from Lee Strasberg, and in time, Lee's wife Paula would become a major influence on Marilyn as her new drama coach. Marilyn also began to associate with New York's literary set, which led to her re-acquaintance with the playwright Arthur Miller, whom she had originally met in 1951. Although she was still spending some time with Joe DiMaggio, Marilyn and Miller soon began a secret affair.

Throughout 1955, Marilyn had been involved in a protracted legal dispute with Fox over contractual obligations but, in early 1956, she returned to Hollywood to work on the film *Bus Stop*, having secured a much improved contract with Fox, which included an approved list of directors with whom she would work.

As soon as filming was completed on *Bus Stop*, Marilyn returned to New York to be reunited with Arthur Miller, who had by this time obtained a divorce from his wife. The couple quickly announced plans to marry, and hoped to travel to England together for their honeymoon, where Marilyn planned to film *The Sleeping Prince* with Laurence Olivier, and Miller would assist in the production of his play *A View from the Bridge*. There was, however, some doubt over whether Miller would be granted a passport, as he had been under investigation by the House UnAmerican Activities Committee, regarding alleged former Communist links. Despite this, on 29 June, the couple were married in White Plains, New York and, within two weeks, having received his passport, Miller and Marilyn were London-bound. The Millers' time in London was not an altogether happy one. Marilyn and Olivier did not get on well, and problems were also

beginning to surface in her new marriage. Meanwhile, *Bus Stop* was released to high praise, but Marilyn was upset to find that her best scenes had been cut from the movie.

Back in the U.S. in 1957, Marilyn decided to take time off from filming, but the year would prove to be far from relaxing. Reviews of *The Sleeping Prince*, which had now been re-titled *The Prince and the Showgirl*, did little to improve matters, and Marilyn's association with Milton Greene was swiftly terminated. Soon afterwards, Miller was convicted for contempt by the House UnAmerican Activities Committee and, later that year, following an ectopic pregnancy, Marilyn took an overdose of sleeping tablets, but survived, after being discovered by her husband. She returned to work the following year, to star in the hit comedy *Some Like it Hot* with Tony Curtis and Jack Lemmon, but once again, filming was a difficult experience for everyone involved, as both Marilyn's health and her marriage continued to deteriorate.

After some time to recuperate from another miscarriage, Marilyn began work on her next movie, *Let's Make Love*, in late 1959, but the film would ultimately receive more publicity for Marilyn's affair with co-star Yves Montand than for any cinematic merit, and it seemed that she was beginning to lose the sparkle that she had brought to so many of her performances.

By 1960, Marilyn had become highly dependent upon her psychoanalyst Dr Greenson, and the drugs that he was prescribing but, once again, she was required to move on to another project almost as soon as *Let's Make Love* was completed. For the last few years, Arthur Miller had been working his short story *The Misfits* into a workable screenplay as a vehicle for Marilyn, and shooting finally commenced in July. However, by this point their marriage was in disarray and, with filming taking place in the heat of the Nevada Desert, it was not long before Marilyn became ill once more. She rallied, and completed *The Misfits* by the end of 1960 but, by the time of its release early the next year, she and Arthur Miller had been divorced. Shortly afterwards, depressed and exhausted, Marilyn was briefly admitted to a psychiatric hospital, at which point Joe DiMaggio made a welcome return into her life.

Marilyn then decided to return to live in Hollywood, settling in a new home in Brentwood, California, with her housekeeper Eunice Murray. She is thought to have enjoyed brief affairs with Frank Sinatra, Robert Kennedy and the President, John F. Kennedy at this time. Although Marilyn seemed to be starting anew, by early 1962 she was seeing Dr Greenson on a daily basis, and he seemed to be exerting increasing control over her life, but with few noticeable positive effects.

In April, Marilyn began work on *Something's Got to Give*, but the production was massively delayed by her persistent lateness and absenteeism, and within a matter of weeks she had been fired. She retreated to her new home whilst negotiations continued with Fox, who agreed to re-hire her on 1 August but, tragically she was never to complete the film. Just days later, on 5 August, Greenson and Murray discovered Marilyn's naked, lifeless body, face down on her bed. She had died of an overdose of sedatives.

Whilst the precise circumstances of Marilyn's death have never been fully established, much is known about how this remarkable woman lived her life, both on screen and behind the scenes, and she will certainly live on in the hearts and minds of her fans for ever.

Opposite and below: Marilyn could present many public faces, including the glamorous femme fatale (*opposite*) and the sophisticated woman, married to a world-renowned playwright, who was starring opposite one of the world's most famous Shakespearian actors (*below*).

IMAGES *of* MARILYN
MONROE

Marilyn discovered!

Opposite and right: Norma Jeane secured her first film contract in 1946 with 20th Century Fox, and soon afterwards adopted the name Marilyn Monroe. As a public relations exercise, the studio decided to circulate the story that Marilyn had been discovered whilst babysitting for a Hollywood casting director. The story was untrue, but provided the opportunity for some wholesome publicity photographs.

Lights, camera, action...

Above: Marilyn was signed up for six months on a salary of $75 a week, after which Fox decided to extend her contract to a year. During this time she appeared in two films, *Scudda Hoo! Scudda Hay!*, and *Dangerous Years* but, at the end of the year, the studio decided to let her go. Nevertheless, Marilyn had gained her first experience in front of the cameras, and was now set on the path to Hollywood stardom.

Opposite: Marilyn was undeterred when Fox decided against renewing her contract and, in addition to resuming her modelling work, she continued to audition for film roles whenever possible. Dedicated to her chosen career and keen to improve her prospects, she also continued to attend classes in acting, singing and dancing, all the while attempting to extend her Hollywood contacts.

A model pupil

Opposite: Marilyn in a promotional shot for *Ladies of the Chorus*. She had returned to modelling, but continued to pursue her dream, and in 1948 she was signed by Columbia Pictures, who gave her a co-starring role in the musical *Ladies of the Chorus*.

Left: Marilyn pictured reading a script with coach Helena Sorell. During the filming of *Ladies of the Chorus* Marilyn fell for her vocal coach Fred Karger, but her feelings were not reciprocated, and she was devastated when he refused to marry her. She did, however, form a close bond with her drama teacher, Natasha Lytess, who would go on to become Marilyn's personal acting coach and friend.

Chorus girls

Left: Although *Ladies of the Chorus* was still a low-budget B-movie, it was Marilyn's biggest role up to that point, and the film also provided her with the opportunity to sing for the first time on screen.

Marilyn sang two numbers, 'Anyone Can See I Love You' and 'Every Baby Needs a Da Da Daddy'. Whilst the film itself received fairly poor reviews, she was favourably noticed by the critics.

Love interest

Opposite: Marilyn's love interest in the movie was Randy Carroll, played by Rand Brooks, and the tale was one of love bridging the social divide between their characters.

Left: When *Ladies of The Chorus* was released, Marilyn was understandably thrilled at the prospect of seeing her name up in lights at the movie theatres; however, deep down she wished that she had adopted the name Jean Monroe which was closer to her own name.

Star quality

Right: At the end of her six months with Columbia, they too decided not to renew her contract but by now Marilyn had made an important contact in the form of top Hollywood agent Johnny Hyde, who seemed to see something in Marilyn that the studios had until now overlooked.

Opposite: Marilyn in a scene from *Ladies of the Chorus*. Whilst the film did not bring Marilyn overnight success, it gave her a well-deserved sense of personal achievement, and hinted at the star quality that she possessed.

Love Happy

Opposite and above: With Johnny Hyde's support and connections, Marilyn's career prospects were much improved, and she soon landed a small part in the Marx Brothers film *Love Happy*, for United Artists. Groucho is said to have asked for 'a young lady who can walk by me in such a manner as to arouse my elderly libido and cause smoke to issue from my ears'. Marilyn fitted the bill and, although the role was again little more than a bit part, appearing with such well-established stars certainly helped to raise her profile, and it would not be long before her own talent for comedy was recognised.

Looking the part

Opposite and right: In addition to taking acting lessons, Marilyn had also learned about fashion, make-up and poise, as revealed by these contrasting publicity shots.

Finding herself without a studio contract once more, she continued to support herself by modelling and, in 1949, she posed naked for photographer Tom Kelly. As a still-aspiring starlet, this passed unnoticed at the time but, a few years later, when the nude photograph of Marilyn was discovered on a calendar, it would spark controversy.

Just the ticket?

Left: Two years had now passed since the end of Marilyn's first contract with 20th Century Fox but, soon after her appearance in *Love Happy* for United Artists, Fox selected her for a role in the musical Western *A Ticket To Tomahawk*. Marilyn's part as a chorus girl was again rather small, but it seemed like a step in the right direction for the budding actress, and perhaps an indication that the studios were beginning to see her potential.

However, Fox had recently released the comedy Western *The Beautiful Blonde from Bashful Bend*, starring Betty Grable and, as a result of that film's poor reception, *A Ticket To Tomahawk* would suffer from a lack of promotion.

Glamour girl

Opposite: Although the movie *A Ticket To Tomahawk* was not heavily promoted, Fox continued to release numerous publicity shots of Marilyn, which were important in developing and maintaining her profile.

Left: Marilyn in *A Ticket To Tomahawk* with Dan Dailey and her fellow chorus girls.

Cheesecake queen

Opposite: Marilyn had first been discovered by photographer David Conover in 1945 whilst working in a munitions factory when he was assigned to take pictures of women engaged in war work. As her acting career gathered momentum, she continued to be a favourite pin-up with members of the armed forces. In 1950, the newspaper for U.S. troops, *Stars and Stripes*, bestowed on her the title 'Miss Cheesecake', and she was also voted as 'the present all GIs would like to find in their Christmas stocking'.

Above: In addition to posing for 'cheesecake' photographs, Marilyn often supplemented her income in the early years by modelling for pin-up artists such as Earl Moran.

The Asphalt Jungle

Right: Marilyn and Sam Jaffe in *The Asphalt Jungle.* In 1950, with Johnny Hyde acting as her agent, Marilyn was to make her first appearance in a high-profile movie, John Huston's *The Asphalt Jungle*, for MGM.

Her part as Angela was still relatively small, consisting of just three scenes, but she attracted favourable reviews from the critics, and Hollywood finally began to sit up and take notice.

Opposite: Marilyn with Louis Calhern, who played the part of her lover, the crooked lawer, Alonzo D. Emmerich. John Huston had decided against casting established movie stars in the film, which gave Marilyn the opportunity to shine.

All About Eve

Opposite and left: Following Johnny Hyde's advice, Marilyn was beginning to realise the importance of working with talented directors and, fortunately, her role in *The Asphalt Jungle* brought her to the attention of director Joseph Mankiewicz. He decided to cast her in his next movie for Fox, *All About Eve*, in which she played the role of Claudia Caswell, an aspiring actress.

The film, which starred Bette Davis and Anne Baxter, went on to great succeses on its release in 1950, receiving fourteen Academy Award nominations, and winning Best Movie and Best Director.

A long-term contract

Opposite and above: At this photoshoot Marilyn began by performing her exercise routine for the cameras, showing that she was in good physical shape, and then lay on the grass in a more provocative pose. As she had now appeared in two highly acclaimed movies, Johnny Hyde was at last able to secure her a long-term contract with Fox, which gave her the security of a salary. However, in 1951, he was to die of a heart attack, leaving Marilyn without an agent and facing an uncertain future. Hyde had been deeply in love with his protégée and, knowing that he was suffering from heart disease, he had proposed marriage on numerous occasions, offering Marilyn financial security in the event of his death. Not being in love with him, she had always refused. It was a decision that she may well have regretted, as Hyde's family were quick to eject her from his home and repossess all he had bought her.

As Young as You Feel

Above: Still mourning Hyde's death, Marilyn was given a part in *As Young as You Feel*, in which she played a young secretary. During filming she would be introduced to the playwright Arthur Miller for the first time.

Opposite: Marilyn appeared in several small roles for Fox in 1951, and was also loaned to RKO to work on Fritz Lang's *Clash by Night*. The film gave her the opportunity to prove her ability as a serious actress and, as she was beginning to become something of a box-office draw, she was given a billing above the film's title. However, she continued to pose for pin-up photographs, on this occasion a Valentine picture for U.S. troops.

We're Not Married

Opposite: Marilyn alongside David Wayne in 1952's romantic comedy *We're Not Married*. The film featured such established names as Fred Allen, Zsa Zsa Gabor and Ginger Rogers, but a part was specifically created for Marilyn on account of her rapidly increasing popularity.

Left: Another Valentine glamour shot. Despite her burgeoning career, Marilyn still considered such photo opportunities important.

Don't Bother to Knock

Opposite: In 1952 Marilyn was given her first leading role opposite Richard Widmark in *Don't Bother to Knock*. It was a serious dramatic part in which she played a maladjusted, abusive babysitter which, despite provoking mixed reactions, suggested that she could carry a film in a starring role.

Right: Marilyn helps out in a campaign to highlight the importance of being careful with fireworks before the 4 July celebrations. Marilyn's figure looks almost boyish here compared to the iconic images of the much more voluptuous Marilyn Monroe at the height of her career.

Beware of Danger
JULY 4th.

Blonde bombshell

Above: Having starred as the dramatic lead in *Don't Bother to Knock*, Marilyn soon found herself returned to lighter, comedic roles, typically playing an attractive, dizzy blonde. It was an image that she would come to feel trapped by as she yearned to be taken seriously as an actress, and one which was perhaps harder to shake off as she continued to pose for pin-up style photographs.

Opposite: Marilyn was always concerned with her appearance, both on and off set but, as her career progressed, her obsession with looking just right would often lead to her being late on set.

Monkey Business

Left: In 1952, Marilyn featured in the screwball comedy *Monkey Business*, which starred Cary Grant and Ginger Rogers.

During filming she was taken ill with appendicitis, but was determined to complete the movie before receiving treatment. At the same time, Marilyn faced a potentially career-damaging scandal, when a nude photo taken of her in 1949 was published in a calendar.

The executives at 20th Century Fox initially planned to deny that it was her, but Marilyn thought that honesty would be the best policy, and so gave an interview to a journalist explaining her actions. Far from provoking outrage, most of Marilyn's fans were sympathetic, and pictures from the shoot would go on to be used in the first edition of *Playboy* magazine.

Right: Marilyn happily signs an autograph for a fan.

Marilyn and Joe

Opposite: Baseball star Joe DiMaggio visiting Marilyn on the set of *Monkey Business*. The pair met for the first time just days after the story of Marilyn's nude photographs was broken to the press, and they were soon to be romantically linked.

Above: A contented Marilyn relaxes in the sunshine. Marilyn was pleasantly surprised by Joe's reserved demeanour, and welcomed the security he offered.

Marilyn's talent revealed

Left: Marilyn's next film project was *Niagara*, in which she would star with Joseph Cotten, as a woman plotting to murder her husband. Some of Marilyn's sexually-charged scenes outraged members of the Women's Clubs of America, and had to be re-edited, but the movie certainly confirmed Marilyn's talent.

Around this time, Joe DiMaggio also began to resent some of Marilyn's more revealing publicity shots.

Opposite: The publicity machine was rarely at rest and here Marilyn is pictured in hospital, fully made-up, while recovering from her appendectomy. She is holding a get-well card from Joe.

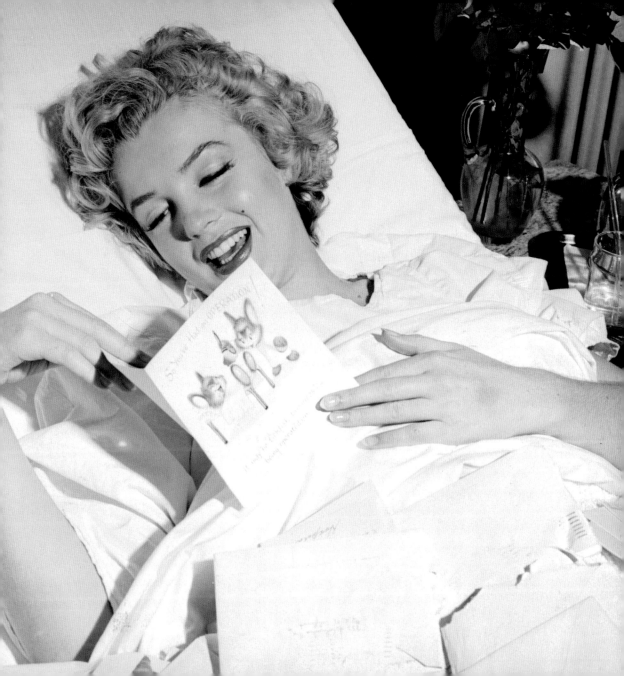

Niagara

Opposite: Marilyn with the director of *Niagara*, Henry Hathaway, who was renowned for losing his temper and raising his voice at actors on set. However, when it came to Marilyn, Hathaway was very protective of his star, and seemed to bring out the best in her.

The movie was released in early 1953, and was a massive commercial success, going on to take over five times its production cost at the box office.

A highly polished performance

Opposite and left: By the time of *Niagara's* release, Marilyn was busy working on her next movie, *Gentlemen Prefer Blondes*, playing showgirl Lorelei Lee, in a role originally intended for Betty Grable. By now, Marilyn was earning over $1,000 per week, but that was nothing compared to her co-star Jane Russell, who could easily command ten times that amount.

The director of the film was Howard Hawks, with whom Marilyn had worked on *Monkey Business*, but in this film he seemed to elicit a more highly polished performance from her.

Gentlemen Prefer Blondes

Above: Marilyn worked hard on both her acting and her dancing for the film, but her insecurites over her ability and appearance seemed to increase around this time, and she was frequently late onto the set as a result. Co-star Jane Russell soon recognised the problem and would support Marilyn by collecting her from her dressing room. Marilyn also sought constant reassurance from her drama coach Natasha Lytess (*above*), which came to infuriate directors and fellow actors alike.

Opposite: Marilyn with Tommy Noonan as playboy Gus Esmond in a scene from *Gentlemen Prefer Blondes*.

Diamonds Are a Girl's Best Friend

Above: Marilyn and Jane Russell in a scene from *Gentlemen Prefer Blondes*. The film famously featured Marilyn performing the song 'Diamonds Are a Girl's Best Friend' but, in reality, the actress did not own a great deal of expensive jewellery.

Opposite: Marilyn's own rags to riches tale came into question when it was revealed that she was not actually an orphan as Fox had suggested and that, for several years, her mother had actually been receiving treatment at a series of mental hospitals. However, once again, Marilyn's public was sympathetic.

Marilyn wins an award

Opposite: Marilyn with her stand-in from *Gentlemen Prefer Blondes*, Irene Crosby. The film was a great success upon its release, and Marilyn was rewarded with *Photoplay* magazine's Best Actress award in 1953.

Above: Jane Russell was able to help Marilyn in her performance in *Gentlemen Prefer Blondes* but, being married to an ex-football player herself, she was also able to offer Marilyn advice as to how to cope with Joe DiMaggio. DiMaggio had only recently retired from playing baseball and Marilyn was unsure as to whether she should marry him.

How to Marry a Millionaire

Opposite: Marilyn as the short-sighted Pola Debevoise in *How to Marry a Millionaire*. Marilyn was now becoming hot property and, just days after the completion of *Gentlemen Prefer Blondes*, she was to begin filming *How to Marry a Millionaire*, with Betty Grable and Lauren Bacall. Despite being exhausted by her schedule, and concerned about being typecast as a dumb blonde, Marilyn was to prove a talented comedic actress.

Above: Marilyn pictured giving an interview to reporter Vern Scott of United Press.

'The thing that made her a star'

Opposite and left: How to Marry a Millionaire, scripted by Nunnally Johnson, was a sophisticated comedy in which three single women, tired of dating, plan to hook a millionaire each. Much of the comedy in the film was generated by Marilyn's character who was very short-sighted but refused to wear glasses declaring, 'Men aren't attentive to girls who wear glasses.' Although her nerves and habitual lateness made working relationships difficult, director Jean Negulesco would later say 'She may have been late and difficult at times, but in the end I adored her because she was a pure child who had this "something" that God gave her... It's the thing that made her a star.'

Marilyn, Bacall and Bogart

Opposite and above: Marilyn at a party to celebrate the opening of *How to Marry a Millionaire*, which was also attended by co-star Lauren Bacall and her husband, Humphrey Bogart (*above*). During filming, reports had circulated that Marilyn and the movie's other established star, Betty Grable, had failed to get on, but they were actually to become good friends.

Appearing with Jack Benny

Left: While publicising *How to Marry a Millionaire*, Marilyn had appeared with the experienced comedian Jack Benny, and the two of them were soon to become close friends. In September 1953, Marilyn appeared live on his television show, where she performed in a comedy sketch with him, and gave a rendition of 'Bye Bye Baby'.

Opposite: Jack and Marilyn enjoying a night out together.

Waiting for an answer

Opposite: By 1953, Joe DiMaggio was hoping to marry Marilyn, but she remained undecided, partly because he did not share her love of art and literature, but most importantly because she was not willing to abandon her hard-earned career to become a housewife. She is pictured reading some of theatre-director Max Reinhardt's original manuscripts, which she had recently purchased. The acquisition sparked some criticism by members of the press who believed it should be donated to a university library.

Above: Marilyn's next movie was *River of No Return*, which was filmed in Canada in 1953. The experience was physically demanding, requiring her and co-star Robert Mitchum to spend long periods soaked in water, but Marilyn never seemed to mind donning a swimsuit for the photographers.

Break a leg...

Opposite: Whilst filming *River of No Return*, Marilyn was to fall and injure her leg, but this was not the only problem she faced on the shoot. She she was still trying to reconcile her feelings for Joe, who had travelled to be with her in Canada, and the director, Otto Preminger, had also banned Marilyn's drama coach, Natasha Lytess from the set due to her interference.

Additionally, Marilyn was torn over her next project for Fox, *The Girl in Pink Tights*, which she was due to begin work on as soon as *River of No Return* was completed.

Charles Feldman, who was acting as Marilyn's agent, was worried that she was beginning to be overworked and overexposed, and wished to negotiate a better contract for her.

Left: Marilyn in a publicity shot from 1953, wearing a gown that she had previously worn in *Niagara*.

Marilyn makes a new conquest

Opposite: Marilyn with Tommy Rettig, who also featured in *River of No Return*. Initially Tommy avoided Marilyn off set, apparently on the advice of his priest, but he could not resist the urge to meet Joe DiMaggio, and relations with Marilyn soon improved.

Above: Marilyn endures a little discomfort as she prepares for a photoshoot to highlight fire safety during the Independence Day celebrations.

Newlyweds...

Opposite and above: With Joe DiMaggio taking more of an interest in Marilyn's career, she finally accepted his proposal of marriage and, in January 1954, now that she was suspended by Fox, the couple took the opportunity to get married. The short ceremony took place in San Francisco, and was meant to be conducted in secret, but Marilyn had informed Fox of her intentions earlier that day, and the press and fans turned out in droves to greet the happy couple. The publicity also caused Fox to relent, and they asked Marilyn to come back to work at the end of the month.

Japan and Korea

Left: Fox were still intent on getting Marilyn to appear in *The Girl in Pink Tights*, but now, having seen the script, she was even more determined not to accept the part. As a result, Fox immediately put her back on suspension, which gave her the time to accompany her new husband on a visit to Japan.

Joe had been asked to open the Japanese baseball season, but he hoped that the trip would otherwise be free of public engagements, and would effectively be an extension of their honeymoon. However, Marilyn had other ideas, and opted to visit the U.S. troops in Korea (*opposite*), much to Joe's disapproval.

Entertaining the troops

Opposite and left: Since her earliest days as a pin-up, Marilyn had valued the support of the troops, and did not hesitate to accept the invitation to entertain them in Korea, despite her husband's misgivings.

She performed ten shows during her four-day tour of the country, and went down a storm, but unfortunately Marilyn's choice of attire was not best suited to the freezing conditions, and she was to suffer from a bout of pneumonia soon afterwards.

Working abroad and at home

Opposite: While in Korea, Marilyn not only sang for the troops, but offered her help in the mess hall.

Right: Whilst Marilyn and Joe were away, back at home Charles Feldman was continuing to negotiate with Fox, hoping to secure her an improved contract.

Marilyn not only wanted a pay rise, but wished to approve her scripts, cinematographer and director before accepting a role.

The main attraction

Opposite: Marilyn was invariably the centre of attention wherever she went. Here she is pictured on her visit to Japan in February 1954. On this trip Marilyn tried hard to allow the spotlight to fall on Joe but her fame, coupled with her naturally more flamboyant personality, made this difficult to achieve.

Above: Marilyn with Jacques Sernas, Sammy Davis Jr, Milton Greene and Mel Tormé. By now Marilyn was an established star and a famous face on Hollywood's celebrity social circuit, but she was still on the salary that had been negotiated in 1951, before her rise to stardom, and was seeking greater consultation over the movies she appeared in.

A triumphant return

Above: Back in Hollywood Marilyn and actor Alan Ladd, pictured at the *Photoplay* awards. Marilyn remained suspended from work, but she still had plenty to smile about, having been voted Most Popular Film Actress of 1953 at an awards ceremony hosted by *Photoplay* magazine.

Opposite: Posing alongside her friend the columnist Sidney Skolsky, Marilyn shows off her award for the cameras.

There's No Business Like Show Business

Right and opposite: Shortly after her return from Japan, Marilyn was pleased to discover that Fox had decided to drop *The Girl in Pink Tights*, but she was to begin work on *There's No Business Like Show Business*, with contractual negotiations still under way.

Her role in the film was a supporting one, but Fox had offered to give her the lead in *The Seven Year Itch*, with a large fee in addition to her salary. The studio also agreed that Marilyn would not be obliged to perform in more than two films per year, but they were unwilling to concede to her demands for greater creative control, other than to consult her on her choice of drama coach and choreographer. Most of the song and dance routines in the film were developed by Robert Alton, but Marilyn was able to work with Jack Cole, with whom she had successfully collaborated while making *Gentlemen Prefer Blondes*.

'After You Get What You Want...'

Left: Marilyn with fellow star Johnny Ray on the set of *There's No Business Like Show Business*. She is pictured in the elaborate costume that she wore whilst performing the song 'After You Get What You Want You Don't Want It'.

Despite appearances, Marilyn was reported to be emotional and lethargic during filming and, after fainting on set, rumours began to circulate that she might be pregnant. In fact, she was still recovering from her recent illness which had begun in Japan, but it is thought that her intake of sleeping pills was also beginning to take its toll at this time.

Opposite: Marilyn and Joe DiMaggio smile for photographers during a dinner soon after their marriage. While Marilyn actively enjoyed the attentions of the press, in general Joe preferred to have Marilyn's undivided attention and did not welcome such intrusions.

End of a relationship

Opposite: Marilyn with her drama coach Natasha Lytess. Despite the fact that Marilyn had long relied upon Natasha for support, they had fallen out over Marilyn's refusal to work on *The Girl in Pink Tights* and, after *The Seven Year Itch*, they would no longer work together.

Above: Marilyn visiting actress Merle Oberon and director Henry Koster on the set of their latest film.

Male attention...

Opposite: Marilyn proudly displays a photograph of Joe on her vanity table. Although Marilyn had told reporters that she and Joe DiMaggio were planning to start a family in the near future, just months after their marriage it seemed that their relationship was already in trouble. Joe disliked all the male attention that Marilyn was receiving and still wished that she would give up her career. Marilyn left for New York to begin filming *The Seven Year Itch* without her husband, but he was to follow in a matter of days.

Above: Marilyn out on the town with Fox founder Joe Schenck and columnist Walter Winchell, who was a friend of Joe DiMaggio.

The Seven Year Itch

Left: Director Billy Wilder had adapted the film *The Seven Year Itch* from the Broadway play and, although it was less risqué than the original, with the action set during a heatwave, the movie still allowed for Marilyn to wear some fairly revealing attire.

The plot concerns a husband left at home alone, who, with his wife and son away on holiday, begins to fantasize about 'The Girl' (Marilyn) who is renting a neighbouring apartment.

Opposite: Marilyn with director Wilder and co-star Tom Ewell.

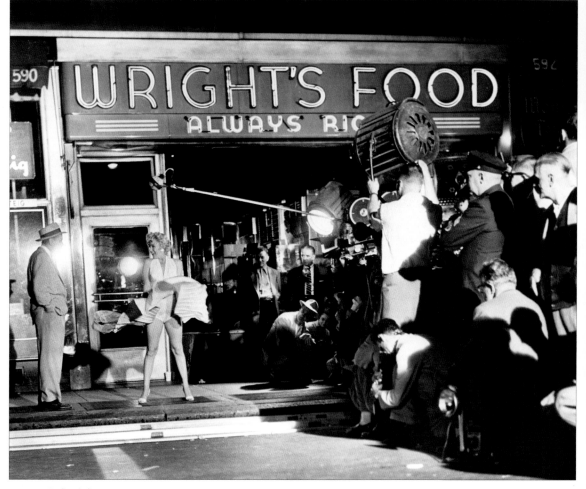

An iconic image

Opposite and above: Marilyn's part called for her to be at once innocent and effortlessly sexy, something with which she would become synonymous, both on and off screen, and in what is almost certainly the most memorable scene of the film, her pleated white skirt is blown upwards as she stands on an air vent. The image would go on to become one of the most iconic of Marilyn's career, but the filming of the scene, which was attended by crowds of cheering men, outraged Joe DiMaggio. Ironically, the scene originally filmed on the streets of New York, later had to be re-shot on a soundstage owing to problems with the sound and light and so Joe had been needlessly upset.

The calm before the storm

Above: A relaxed moment with Joe, Marilyn and actor David Wayne, backstage at the Martin Beck Theater, where Wayne was starring in *The Teahouse of the August Moon*. Unfortunately, after Marilyn had filmed the famous skirt sequence, she and Joe had a terrible argument and he was to leave New York.

Opposite: Marilyn and co-star Tom Ewell in a publicity shot for *The Seven Year Itch*.

Blonde meets brunette

Opposite: Marilyn with Italian actress Gina Lollobrigida, who had recently starred in *Beat the Devil* opposite Humphrey Bogart. La Lollo, as she was known, had commented on how different she was from Marilyn, prompting columnist Earl Wilson to unite them in New York.

Above: Marilyn and Tom Ewell pictured sharing a joke. Several leading men had auditioned for the role of Richard Sherman, but Ewell had the advantage of having played the part on Broadway.

Troubled times

Above and opposite: Even before *The Seven Year Itch* was in the can, Marilyn's and Joe's relationship was at breaking point and, by October 1954, it was revealed that she had filed for divorce on the grounds of 'mental cruelty', no longer able to cope with DiMaggio's jealousy and controlling persona. The announcement was made by Marilyn's attorney, Jerry Giesler, with Marilyn unable to speak as she held back the tears.

Divorced from Joe DiMaggio

Left: Marilyn testified before the court at her divorce hearing dressed as if in mourning. She had truly loved her husband and was devastated that the marriage had not worked out as she had hoped. However, in a statement issued by her attorney, Jerry Giesler, the divorce was described as a 'regrettable necessity'.

Opposite: Marilyn signing the divorce papers. The judge granted the separation, but it would not legally come into effect until the following October, one year later.

A brave face

Above: Marilyn surrounded by photographers and fans as she leaves the divorce court with Jerry Giesler in October 1954. Despite the divorce, Marilyn and Joe were to remain close friends right to the end of her life, which would spark rumours of a possible reunion on several occasions. Shortly after the split, for instance, Marilyn was taken ill with endometriosis, and Joe kept an almost constant vigil at her bedside.

Opposite: Marilyn is pictured just before going into hospital, and must have been in severe discomfort, but she was still able to find a smile for the camera.

Making plans...

Above: Although Marilyn was still on contract to Fox, she craved greater artistic control over her career, and began to discuss the possibility of setting up her own production company with the photographer Milton Greene, who was also hoping to move into the movie business. She is pictured here with Greene at the Beverly Hills Hotel, being interviewed by Maria Romero.

What lies ahead?

Above: Whilst there, Marilyn also had her fortune told by the palm-reader Hassan, who predicted that she would have two children. Marilyn desperately wanted to be a mother, but unfortunately it was never to be.

Platinum blonde

Opposite and right: At the end of
1954, Marilyn left California for New
York where, in January 1955, she was
to announce the formation of Marilyn
Monroe Productions, which she had
founded with Milton Greene.

At the same time, Marilyn was
to unveil her 'new', platinum blonde
image, in preparation for playing
Jean Harlow in a film of the actress's
life story.

However, the press could see
little evidence of a transformation
and, in deciding to focus on this, the
launch of Marilyn's new production
company was barely noticed.

A dispute with Fox

Opposite: Although the newspapers had
paid little attention to Marilyn's bid for
independence, the move did not pass
unnoticed by 20th Century Fox and their
legal team, who reminded her that she
remained tied to an exclusive contract with
them for the next few years. In response,
Marilyn and her lawyers were to highlight
a number of contractual discrepancies and
unfulfilled obligations on Fox's part,
including the non-payment of her fee for
The Seven Year Itch. The ensuing legal
dispute would take most of the year to
resolve, but Marilyn returned to Hollywood
early in 1955 in order to reshoot a scene
for the film.

Right: Whilst in New York, Marilyn found
the time to become involved with various
charity campaigns, such as this one for
arthritis.

New York socialite

Left: Marilyn at the opening of Tennessee Williams' play, *Cat on a Hot Tin Roof*. Now residing with Milton Greene and his wife in Connecticut, Marilyn was introduced to their social circle, and was soon attending numerous parties, premieres and charity functions.

It seemed as if her acting career had been temporarily put on hold, but behind the scenes she was concentrating on developing her technique by studying with Lee Strasberg at his Actors Studio.

Opposite: At the premiere of *East of Eden*, starring James Dean, Marilyn raised money for charity by working as an usherette.

Just good friends

Above: When Marilyn attended the New York premiere of *The Seven Year Itch*, she arrived with former husband Joe DiMaggio on her arm and, once again, the press began to talk of a reconciliation. However, Marilyn insisted that they were just good friends.

Opposite: In 1953, the Jewelry Academy had voted Marilyn the 'Best Friend a Diamond Ever Had'; now two years later she appeared at a function for the Jeweler's Association dressed from head to toe in precious stones.

Announcing a new movie

Opposite: In early 1956, Marilyn and Laurence Olivier held a press conference at New York's Plaza Hotel, where they revealed their plans to bring Terence Rattigan's play *The Sleeping Prince* to the big screen.

Marilyn was desperate to be taken seriously as an actress and hoped that working alongside the great Olivier might help her to achieve this objective.

Left: Marilyn dancing with writer Truman Capote, whom she had first met in 1950, the same year that she had made the acquaintance of playwright Arthur Miller. Now that she was associating with the New York literary set, it would not be long until their paths crossed once more.

Wardrobe malfunction

Opposite and right: During the press conference with Laurence Olivier, the strap on Marilyn's dress broke, threatening not only to reveal her body, but also to undermine the serious image she was attempting to cultivate. Olivier believed that the 'accident' was a publicity stunt but, either way, it certainly grabbed the attention of the assembled reporters.

Meanwhile, Marilyn had been continuing to negotiate with Fox, in the hope of resolving their dispute, and she was soon to return to Hollywood with an unprecedented deal, which included a percentage of film takings and the approval of her scripts, cinematographers and directors.

Back to business

Opposite: Marilyn's successful challenge to the traditional studio system marked her out, in the words of *Time* magazine, as a 'shrewd businesswoman', and she certainly looked the part in her tailored suit.

Above: Marilyn's new contract also gave her the permission to work on one film a year independently of Fox, and it was soon announced that *The Sleeping Prince* would be produced for Warner Brothers. Here she is pictured with Jack Warner, who seems overjoyed at the prospect.

A court appearance

Left: Back in Hollywood, having settled her contract with Fox, Marilyn was preparing to start work on her next film, but first she had some other legal matters to attend to: a court case for having been caught driving without a licence in 1954. She was found guilty, and fined $56.

Whilst Marilyn had not worked on a film for over a year, her drama coach, Natasha Lytess, had remained on Fox's payroll, and now that Marilyn was about to resume her acting career, Natasha assumed that her services would be in demand once more. However, to her surprise and dismay, she found that Lee Strasberg's wife, Paula, had been brought in to replace her.

Opposite: Marilyn with actor James Cagney at a Beverly Hills party hosted by *Look* magazine. Despite her break from filming, Marilyn's time in New York and her triumphant return to Hollywood had considerably raised her profile.

Bus Stop

Left and opposite: Before work on *The Sleeping Prince* got under way, Marilyn began her next film for 20th Century Fox, *Bus Stop*. It told the story of a bar-room singer, Cherie, who falls for the charms of a cowboy, Bo. Marilyn was to play the part of Cherie, whilst Don Murray was selected as the leading man.

Director Joshua Logan was initially sceptical about Marilyn's ability as an actress, and was also concerned that she might be very demanding to work with, particularly as she had complained about her costumes before shooting even began. However, after she picked out some clothes that even he agreed were more suited to her character, his fears were allayed.

At first, Logan refused to allow drama coach Paula Strasberg on set, but he soon relented, and even made exceptions for Marilyn's frequent lateness.

The fairest of them all?

Above: Unfortunately Marilyn's relationship with fellow actors Don Murray and Hope Lange was not as relaxed as that which she enjoyed with director Logan. Tensions were raised when she refused to apologise to Murray after accidentally injuring him during a scene and demanded that Lange's hair be dyed darker than her own.

Exhausted!

Above: Marilyn, Don Murray and Arthur O'Connell, who played the part of Bo's guardian, Virgil Blessing. Filming took place in the mountains of Idaho and in the Arizona Desert, and Marilyn found it an exhausting experience. She also came down with a case of bronchitis, which resulted in her being hospitalised for several days.

Happy Birthday...

Opposite and right: On the occasion of Marilyn's 30th birthday in June 1956, just after the completion of *Bus Stop*, she was to attend a party held by director Joshua Logan. Amongst the assembled guests was President Sukarno of Indonesia, who explained that her films were highly popular in his country.

For several months, Marilyn had been enjoying a quiet romantic affair with the playwright Arthur Miller and, whilst she had been filming *Bus Stop*, he had been in Reno, Nevada, attempting to obtain a divorce from his wife.

As soon as the divorce was granted, Miller returned to New York and, the day after her birthday, Marilyn flew there to join him.

Her lips were sealed...

On her arrival at New York's Idlewild Airport the day after her birthday, Marilyn was happy to pose for photographers with a birthday cake she had been given. She would not be drawn on the subject of her relationship with Arthur Miller, simply blowing reporters a kiss in response to their questions.

Marilyn and Miller were actually planning to visit London, where Miller's play *A View from the Bridge* was due to open, and where Marilyn would begin filming *The Sleeping Prince*. However, because of a previous association with the Communist Party, Miller had recently been called to testify before the UnAmerican Activities Committee, and there was some doubt that his passport application would be successful.

Wedding plans

Opposite and right: Although he was still
waiting for a decision regarding his
passport application, Arthur Miller
revealed his intention to marry Marilyn,
saying that she would be going to London
as his wife, whether or not he was able to
accompany her there.

The press were understandably
excited by the news, but Miller had
known that Marilyn was the girl that he
wanted to marry ever since becoming
reacquainted with her in New York, and
had told his parents so after she had first
visited their home.

Glowing with excitement

Above and opposite: Following Arthur Miller's revelation that he and Marilyn planned to be wed, she had no need to hide the fact from reporters, and could barely contain her excitement as she discussed the matter with them at a press conference in New York. A date had not yet been set, but journalists were informed that the ceremony would be held sometime in July.

144

Married in secret

Opposite and above: Hounded by reporters, Arthur and Marilyn decided to leave New York City for Miller's countryside retreat in Connecticut, but the press were quick to follow them. As a result, the couple conceded a relaxed photocall, where they were to appeal for some peace. However, it was not to be and, on 29 June, journalist Mara Scherbatoff was fatally injured when the car in which she was following Marilyn and Miller struck a tree. Arthur Miller promptly moved the wedding forward to that evening in an attempt to put an end to the media attention, and they were married in secret at a civil ceremony, in White Plains, New York. This was followed by a religious ceremony, held at the home of Miller's agent, Kay Brown.

Mr and Mrs Miller

Above and opposite: Seemingly unperturbed by the tragic car crash that they had witnessed the previous day, newlyweds Arthur and Marilyn set off for a picnic. Secretly however, Marilyn regarded the incident as an ominous sign since it had occurred so very close to their wedding. Marilyn was further distressed by the fact that they were due to leave the U.S. for London in less than two weeks' time but were still waiting to hear if her husband would be granted a passport.

Honeymoon

Opposite: With just days to spare, the news came that Miller's passport had been approved, and the couple could now enjoy their planned trip to London together. Although both of them had work to do in England, they also hoped that they would be able to spend some quality time together, and could treat the trip as their honeymoon.

Right: As they left the U.S. for England, the newlyweds shared a kiss for photographers. By now Marilyn was well used to being in the limelight, but for Miller, the experience was somewhat unsettling.

Welcomed by the Oliviers

Opposite and left: On their arrival in London, Arthur and Marilyn were greeted by Laurence Olivier and his wife, Vivien Leigh, who had starred in the original stage production of *The Sleeping Prince*. Marilyn and Olivier were due to begin work on a film version, which would be the first project for Marilyn Monroe Productions. Both Marilyn and Olivier would star in the film, and he would also be acting as producer and director.

Marilyn saw it as a great opportunity to work with such a highly regarded actor, whilst Olivier hoped that being associated with superstar Marilyn might invigorate his career.

Having been collected at the airport, the Millers and Milton Greene, who had accompanied them, were chauffeured to their rented mansion, Parkside House, which lay just outside of Windsor Great Park. The Oliviers arrived shortly afterwards, providing an opportunity for an impromptu photocall.

The Prince and the Showgirl

Opposite: Although *The Sleeping Prince* would eventually be released as *The Prince and the Showgirl*, filming commenced under the play's original title. Both Marilyn and Olivier were excited about the project, but it would not be long until problems arose.

Marilyn's style of acting, which had been fostered by Lee Strasberg, was completely at odds with that of Olivier and, with Paula Strasberg coaching Marilyn on set, Olivier felt that he was being constantly undermined.

Tensions on set were also exacerbated by Marilyn's habitual lateness, and her faliure to remember her lines, which Olivier saw as deeply unprofessional. All of this served to increase Marilyn's anxiety, which was already causing her sleepless nights. It seemed that she was beginning to become trapped in a vicious circle, whereby she would then rely on alcohol and sleeping tablets in order to cope with her stress. However, somehow Marilyn always seemed to shine for the cameras.

Right: Despite her fame, Marilyn found that in London she could melt into a crowd if she chose to, as she had sometimes done in New York.

A View from the Bridge

Whilst Marilyn had been working on
The Sleeping Prince, Arthur Miller
had been helping with preparations
for the staging of his play, *A View
from the Bridge*.

The play opened at the Comedy
Theatre but, due to objections about
the content of the piece from the
Lord Chamberlain, a licence for
public performance had been
refused. As a result, a private club,
the New Watergate Theatre Club,
had to be hastily formed before
even its author could attend a
performance of the play.

The central theme of *A View
from the Bridge* concerns a man's
betrayal of his friends, which
ultimately leads to his own downfall.
It was a concept that weighed
heavily on Miller's mind throughout
this period, as the UnAmerican
Activities Commitee had asked him
to reveal the names of possible
Communist sympathisers, and he
was still waiting to find out whether
he would be held in contempt of
court for refusing to do so.

Black-tie premiere

Above and opposite: Marilyn and Arthur Miller appeared happy and relaxed at the black-tie opening of *A View from the Bridge*, which they attended with Laurence Olivier and Vivien Leigh. However, beneath the surface, the couple were already beginning to experience difficulties in their relationship. In August, Miller had briefly returned to the U.S. in order to visit his children, which left Marilyn feeling alone and abandoned, whilst he was beginning to find the reality of being married to a sex-symbol and superstar more demanding than he had at first imagined. It seemed as though Miller's idealised view of Marilyn had not taken her anxieties and fallibilities into account. Meanwhile, she had discovered some of his notes, in which she believed that he was expressing regrets about their marriage. It seemed that both of them found it difficult to separate fact from fiction, and their upset was increased further when Marilyn suffered a miscarriage around this time.

Homeward bound...

Left: Marilyn and Miller greet cast members backstage after a performance of *A View from the Bridge*. Despite their busy schedules, the couple attended several theatre perfomances in London, including *South Sea Bubble*, featuring Vivien Leigh, and Brecht's *Caucasian Chalk Circle*.

Opposite: Marilyn waves goodbye from her car as she and her husband prepare to leave London. Their time in England had been full of ups and downs and they were looking forward to returning home. During their stay in London, Marilyn's last movie, *Bus Stop*, had been released to glowing reviews, in which the critics finally seemed to recognize her capabilities as an actress. However, a dramatic and moving monologue, which Marilyn had regarded as her best work, and possibly her best chance of an Oscar nomination, had been cut from the film. Marilyn had seen a rough cut of the movie whilst in England and was naturally upset by the edit. She had hoped that it would finally dispel the myth that she was only capable of portraying a dumb blonde and, moreover, would win Miller's respect.

Goodbye Kisses

Opposite: When Marilyn and Arthur Miller left England to return to the U.S. in November 1956, Laurence Olivier and Vivien Leigh came to see them off at the airport and there were kisses all round for Marilyn. Overall, however, the time in London had not been a very happy one for anyone involved. Marilyn had found Olivier far more distant than when they had previously met in New York, and both couples had been experiencing problems in their relationships. Additionally, Marilyn and Milton Greene had also fallen out, partly because of a mutual distrust between Greene and Arthur Miller and, despite all that he had done to support her, Greene's days at Marilyn Monroe Productions were numbered.

Right: Back in the U.S., Marilyn performed another turn as an usherette, this time at the premiere of Elia Kazan's *Baby Doll*, proceeds from which were to be donated to the Actors Studio.

More awards for Marilyn

Above: Marilyn greets a decoratively costumed soldier at the New York premiere of *The Prince and the Showgirl*. The movie received mixed reviews upon its release, and was not a huge commercial success, but Marilyn was to receive a British Academy Award nomination as Best Foreign Actress for her performance, and it would also win her Italy's David di Donatello Award and the French Crystal Star. Marilyn easily outshone Olivier in the film, and today her performance is widely regarded as being amongst the best of her career.

Opposite: Despite Marilyn's best efforts to be recognised as a serious actress, the studio and many of her fans still preferred to see her in glamorous roles.

Back in New York

Above: Upon her return to the U.S., Marilyn decided to take another break from filming in order to concentrate on repairing her relationship with Arthur Miller. The couple settled in an apartment in New York, where Miller could work, whilst Marilyn set about making it into a home that they could both enjoy. However, she still found the time to attend the occasional social function, such as this April in Paris Ball, where she is pictured with society hostess Elsa Maxwell.

Opposite: Marilyn and Arthur Miller were also determined to try again for a baby, and because of her earlier problems with endometriosis, she began treatment at Doctors Hospital in New York.

Supporting role

Above: Arthur Miller had been indicted on two counts of contempt of Congress by a federal grand jury, and was called to the Federal District Court in Washington. He was facing a possible two-year prison term and massive fines, but was eventually found guilty on just one charge, fined $500 and given a month's suspended sentence. Marilyn had accompanied her husband to Washington to support him, but managed to avoid reporters until the end of the hearing.

Opposite: During this time, Marilyn was delighted to find that she was pregnant again, only to discover a few months later that the pregnancy was once more ectopic and the baby could not be carried to full term. Despite the bad news, she was still able to muster a smile for reporters as she left hospital with her husband at her side.

Testing times

Above and opposite: As a result of her failed pregnancy, Marilyn began to feel increasingly depressed and insecure and, soon afterwards, took an overdose of sleeping tablets. However, she was saved when Miller discovered her and raised the alarm. Miller then attempted to reassure Marilyn of his love for her by beginning work on a screenplay of his short story *The Misfits*, with a view to providing his wife with her next starring role. However, Fox were reluctant to become involved due to Miller's recent political difficulties, and Marilyn was wary that he was simply serving his own interests with the project. Nevertheless, she accompanied her husband to his induction into the National Institute of Arts and Letters in early 1958, and was happy to sign autographs for waiting fans.

Some Like It Hot

Left: Although Marilyn still had a number of films to make for Fox in order to fulfil her contractual obligations, she was still also entitled to appear in movies for other production companies, and so began talks with the Mirisch brothers and United Artists after receiving the script for *Some Like It Hot* from director Billy Wilder. Here Marilyn is pictured in discussion with the president of the Mirisch Company, Harold Mirisch.

Opposite: Set in the 1920s, the film's plot centres around two male musicians who disguise themselves as women in order to hide from gangsters after witnessing the Valentine's Day Massacre.

The male leads were to be played by Tony Curtis and Jack Lemmon, whilst Marilyn was to play the role of Sugar Kane, a ukulele player and singer with the band. Curtis and Lemmon were coached by drag artist Barbette (second left) to help make their performances more ladylike.

Sugar Kane

Opposite and right: Marilyn was initially reluctant to accept the part of Sugar Kane, believing it ridiculous that her character should never discover that the 'girls' played by Curtis and Lemmon were actually men, but she relented after Miller convinced her of the quality of the script.

Although he was convinced that Marilyn was perfect for the role, director Billy Wilder also had some misgivings about working with her again, having directed her in *The Seven Year Itch* and found her lateness and inability to remember her lines exasperating at times.

These were problems that Wilder would have to endure again during the production of *Some Like It Hot* but, once filming was over, Marilyn's performance convinced him that he had made the right decision.

'Too old and too rich...'

Opposite: Director Billy Wilder talks to Marilyn on the set of *Some Like It Hot*. After a promising start, Marilyn was soon back to her old ways and, if anything, Wilder found her even more difficult to work with than he had done before, explaining that he was now 'too old and too rich' to want to work with her again. Marilyn's intake of prescription drugs had increased dramatically by this time, and she was more unreliable than ever.

Above: Marilyn with Tony Curtis in a scene from *Some Like It Hot*. Curtis and Lemmon also found it difficult to work with Marilyn at points. They felt a pressure to be good in every take, no matter how many times the scene was shot, because Billy Wilder would be forced to use the versions in which Marilyn had performed well.

On the road to recovery

Above: Marilyn became pregnant again during the filming of *Some Like It Hot*, but in December 1958 she miscarried this baby too, and avoided the attention of the press whilst she recovered. However, in March 1959 she attended the New York premiere of the film with Arthur Miller, looking happy and well.

Opposite: Marilyn in a publicity shot taken by photographer Frank Powolny for 20th Century Fox. This photograph was one in the same series as that which was later immortalised as a screenprint by the artist Andy Warhol.

It's a wrap...

Left: Wrapped up against the cold, Marilyn arrives at La Guardia Airport on her way to the Chicago premiere of *Some Like It Hot*. Despite all the problems experienced during filming, including costing the production over $200,000 dollars due to her illness and lateness, the film was to prove a massive critical and financial success. As one of the highest-grossing films of 1959, *Some Like It Hot* also set a long-standing box-office record for a comedy, and continues to be regarded as one of Marilyn's best films.

Opposite: In 1959, on account of her endometriosis, which had resulted in a number of ectopic pregnancies and miscarriages, Marilyn was to undergo gynaecological surgery, which it was hoped would finally allow her to have a baby. She was accompanied to hospital by her husband Arthur Miller.

Time and Tide

Above: Marilyn meets the author of *Out of Africa*, Isak Dinesen, also known as Baroness Karen Blixen, at the home of her writer friend Carson McCullers. Around this time, Marilyn was due to begin work on *Time and Tide*, based on novels by the author William Bradford, but Fox accidentally allowed their filming schedule to lapse, failing to realise that Marilyn would no longer be obliged to work on the picture, and that they would still have to pay her as if she had; additionally, Marilyn would then owe the studio one less film.

Opposite: Marilyn looked happy and hopeful as she left New York's Lennox Hill Hospital after her operation, but tragically she would never successfully carry a baby to term.

An early arrival

Right: Flying in from New York, Marilyn arrived uncharacteristically early for a luncheon at 20th Century Fox studios in Hollywood, which was being held in honour of the visiting Russian leader, Nikita Khrushchev. Marilyn's interest in the country stemmed from the fact that she had been learning to act according to the methods of the Soviet actor and director Konstantin Stanislavsky.

Opposite: Having had to concede defeat over the *Time and Tide* project, by now Fox had lined up a new film for Marilyn to begin working on. Originally titled *The Billionaire*, the movie would ultimately be released as *Let's Make Love* but, even before filming began, the venture was beset by difficulties, including the loss of co-star Gregory Peck. Shooting was also delayed as Marilyn became increasingly dependent on alcohol and prescription drugs. She was also unhappy with the original script and, although he was not credited for the work, Arthur Miller was brought in to rewrite it extensively before shooting could commence.

Let's Make Love

Opposite and left: Essentially a comedy
of errors, *Let's Make Love* centres
around a case of mistaken identity,
which occurs during the production of a
satirical show about the life of a
billionaire, Jean-Marc Clément. Hearing
about the show, Clément arrives at a
rehearsal in New York's Greenwich
Village and, with the producers
believing that he is a look-alike, he is
promptly cast in the lead, only to fall for
his blonde co-star, Amanda Dell.

Marilyn played Amanda, whilst
Gregory Peck had by now been replaced
by the French actor and sex-symbol,
Yves Montand.

Cocktails and chemistry

Above: Marilyn with Frankie Vaughan and Yves Montand, her co-stars in *Let's Make Love*, at a cocktail party held to welcome Montand to Hollywood and to introduce him to the American press. Montand, who was touring the U.S. with a one-man show, had been suggested for the role of Jean-Marc Clément by Marilyn's husband, Arthur Miller, and Marilyn and Miller soon became good friends with Montand and his wife Simone Signoret.

Opposite: Marilyn and Montand at the cocktail party. There was an immediate chemistry between them, which was perhaps partly fuelled by Montand's superficial resemblance to Marilyn's former husband Joe DiMaggio.

A public affair

Opposite and above: Despite the friendship that had developed between the two couples, when Miller left for New York to continue writing, and Signoret returned to France, Marilyn and Montand were to become embroiled in a passionate affair. Neither of them expected it to be the start of a lasting relationship however and, despite the affair being widely publicised, neither Miller nor Signoret seemed particularly perturbed. Miller's reaction was almost certainly particularly distressing for Marilyn, who was beginning to feel once again that Miller was becoming increasingly cold and distant, despite the fact that he was still busy working on his adaptation of *The Misfits* for her.

A word of advice

Above and opposite: Marilyn receives advice from the director of *Let's Make Love*, George Cukor. It had become usual for directors and co-stars to become frustrated with Marilyn during filming, but even her relationship with her dance coach, Jack Cole, with whom she had worked since 1953, and who was brought in for the film, was beginning to suffer. However, Cukor at least did not have to contend with on-set interference from Marilyn's drama coach Paula Strasberg, as Marilyn and Paula were no longer getting on at this time.

Losing the magic?

Opposite and right: By now, Marilyn was seeing her psychotherapist, Dr Ralph Greenson, on a regular basis, and in addition to sessions of psychotherapy, Greenson was prescribing various drugs as part of Marilyn's treatment, including tranquillisers and barbiturates. However, Marilyn was continuing to combine her medication with alcohol, and throughout the filming of *Let's Make Love*, her problems with lateness and her failure to remember the script were more apparent than ever. In addition, Marilyn was beginning to appear tired, and seemed to be losing the magic sparkle that she had somehow always managed to produce.

'My Heart Belongs to Daddy'

Above: Soon after work had begun on *Let's Make Love*, filming was halted for several months by a strike instigated by actors and supported by The Writers' Guild. In addition to costing the production valuable time and money, by the time filming recommenced, Marilyn had apparently gained weight, which required various on-set adjustments to her costumes.

Opposite: Although *Let's Make Love* did not prove to be a major success, it was memorable for Marilyn's rendition of Cole Porter's 'My Heart Belongs to Daddy'.

A song and dance man

Above: Marilyn with co-star Yves Montand in a scene from *Let's Make Love*. Unlike his character in the film, Montand was actually a talented singer and dancer, but he was also known for his dramatic roles, and had appeared in Miller's play *The Crucible*, in his native France.

Marilyn wins a Golden Globe

Above: Marilyn poses for photographers as she celebrates the receipt of a Golden Globe Award for 'Best Actress in a Motion Picture Comedy', which was presented for her performance in *Some Like It Hot*.

The Misfits

Above: Almost as soon as filming had finished on *Let's Make Love*, Marilyn and Arthur Miller flew to Nevada to begin location shooting for *The Misfits*. Miller had written the screenplay as a gift for Marilyn, but by now the couple were hardly communicating, and Marilyn believed that her husband was merely attempting to further his own career with the movie. She is pictured here with various cast and crew members, including Miller, Montgomery Clift, Clark Gable and director John Huston.

Opposite: Marilyn was also disappointed with her character, Roslyn, feeling that Miller had simply created her as a superficial and damaged version of herself, and yet he was also exposing aspects of Marilyn's personal life before the cameras and the publlic.

Exhausted again

Left: Marilyn had never enjoyed jumping from one film to another without time to rest and prepare herself, and with hardly a break between this project and her last, the experience was always likely to be a difficult one. However, on-set tensions were intensified by the fact that filming was taking place in the sweltering summer heat in the Nevada Desert, as well as by Marilyn's increasing dependency on drugs and alcohol. She was evidently physically and mentally exhausted by the whole process, and mid-way through the shoot, Marilyn had to be hospitalised for several days.

The last movie

Above: After ten days at the Westside Hospital in Los Angeles, Marilyn returned to Nevada to complete work on *The Misfits*, which would last for about another month. She is pictured in a scene from the film, with her co-star Clark Gable. Neither of them could have known that this would be their last movie.

Opposite: Miller and Marilyn in discussion with director John Huston. Miller agonised over the film, hoping that the material would rival that of his best plays, but he could not reconcile this with his belief that Hollywood movies were essentially a lower art form.

A warm relationship

Opposite and left: Despite all of the on-set difficulties, Marilyn and her co-star Clark Gable got on well during filming but, when Gable suffered a heart attack the day after the movie was finished and, sadly, passed away less than two weeks later, certain sections of the public and press turned on Marilyn and blamed her for his death.

It was suggested that Marilyn had caused Gable undue stress but, whilst she admitted to feeling guilty for having kept him waiting on set so many times, many of her supporters felt that she was being made a scapegoat not just for his death, but for all of the movie's production problems.

Although *The Misfits* has become renowned for its troubled production, and was undoubtedly a tough time for all those involved, both Gable and Marilyn gave brilliant performances.

Living separately

Throughout the filming of *The Misfits*, Marilyn and Miller stayed in separate accommodation and, shortly after Marilyn's return from hospital, the couple announced that they had separated. It was rumoured that Miller had begun an affair with photographer Inge Morath whilst on set, and just a week after filming concluded in early November, Marilyn and Miller revealed their plans to divorce.

Alone again

Above: After completing *The Misfits* in late 1960, Marilyn returned to New York, where, alone on Christmas Eve, she was to receive a bouquet of flowers from her former husband, Joe DiMaggio, which would lead to a rekindling of their friendship. In January 1961, she was divorced from Arthur Miller in Mexico and, that same month, *The Misfits* opened to critical acclaim. Marilyn attended a Broadway preview of the movie with Montgomery Clift, who had also starred in the film, and was careful to avoid Miller, who was also in attendance.

Opposite: Marilyn looking somewhat less glamorous than usual, and seemingly oblivious to the camera. By now her lifestyle was beginning to take its toll and, after her third failed marriage, Marilyn was sinking into depression.

Joe to the Rescue...

Opposite: In February 1961, at the suggestion of Dr Kris, her analyst, Marilyn admitted herself to the Payne-Whitney Clinic, seemingly unaware that it was a psychiatric hospital. Upon realising, Marilyn became highly distressed, and was subsequently restrained and sedated. Three days later, Joe DiMaggio arranged for her to be transferred to the Columbia-Presbyterian Medical Center, and three weeks later, she left to spend time relaxing with Joe in Florida.

Above: Soon afterwards Marilyn was back in hospital for an operation to remove her gall bladder.

World's Favourite Film Star

Opposite: Towards the end of 1961, Marilyn decided to return to Los Angeles, where she was soon enjoying the social swirl of Hollywood parties once more, and was to become romantically involved with Robert Kennedy, after brief dalliances with Frank Sinatra, and reportedly also with Robert's brother, President John F. Kennedy, to whom she would famously sing 'Happy Birthday' the following year.

Meanwhile, Marilyn bought a new apartment in Brentwood, California, which she set about furnishing and, in early 1962, she was presented with a Golden Globe by Rock Hudson, as the World's Favourite Film Star of 1961.

Right: Just weeks later, Marilyn began work on her next movie for Fox, *Something's Got to Give*, with co-star Dean Martin and director George Cukor but, despite seeming to have made a new start, and appearing in good physical shape, Marilyn was now seeing her new psychiatrist Dr Greenson, once, or even twice a day, and she seemed incapable of functioning without his support and the drugs he was prescribing.

As a result, Fox eventually fired Marilyn from the movie, but following high-profile photo-shoots for *Life*, *Vogue* and *Cosmopolitan* magazines, which included some sensational nude shots, the studio reconsidered and agreed to re-hire her on 1 August.

Tragically, however, Marilyn was never to return to the set.

A tragic ending

Left: Much has been written about the last hours of Marilyn's life and there has been a great deal of speculation as to the circumstances surrounding her death. On 4 August 1962, Marilyn spent several hours with her psychiatrist Dr Greenson. He left Marilyn's home in the early evening but had asked Marilyn's housekeeper, Eunice Murray, to stay the night. In the early hours of 5 August, Eunice Murray became concerned that Marilyn's bedroom light was still on, and so called Dr Greenson for assistance. When Greenson arrived, they broke into Marilyn's room, to find her lying on the bed, still clutching the telephone, although it was evident that she had been dead for quite some time.

The autopsy revealed large amounts of barbiturates in her system, and the cause of death was recorded as an overdose, but whether this was accidental, suicide, or even deliberately administered by a third party, remains the subject of speculation.

Joe DiMaggio and Marilyn had apparently been planning to re-marry on 8 August, but instead Joe now found himself attending her funeral, which was held at Westwood Memorial Park, Los Angeles. Joe oversaw the arrangements, inviting only close friends and family, and as he had promised Marilyn years before, he would have flowers delivered to her grave every week, a practice he maintained for over 20 years.

CHRONOLOGY

1926

1 Jun   Marilyn is born Norma Jeane Mortensen in Los Angeles, California

13 Jun   The new baby is left with the neighbouring Bolender family after her mother returns to work

Dec   At her christening, the baby is named Norma Jeane – but she spells her second name with and without the 'e' throughout her childhood

1927

July   The toddler Norma Jeane is nearly suffocated by her grandmother, Della Monroe, who is later admitted to the Metropolitan State Hospital in Norwalk, LA County

23 Aug   Della dies of a heart attack in hospital

1933

Jun   Norma Jeane leaves the Bolenders to live with her mother, Gladys, in North Hollywood

Aug   Gladys obtains a mortgage and they move into a house on Arbol Street, sharing it with an English couple

Oct   Gladys hears that her grandfather, Tilford Hogan, has committed suicide

1934

Jan   Gladys is admitted to a rest home in Santa Monica, having suffered a mental breakdown

1935

Jan   Gladys is committed to the Metropolitan State Hospital in Norwalk, LA County, with a diagnosis of paranoid schizophrenia

Apr   Gladys's estate is assessed as she is no longer able to manage her affairs

1 Jun   Grace McKee becomes responsible for liquidating Gladys's estate

13 Sept   Norma Jeane is placed in the Los Angeles Orphans Society Home

1936

26 Feb   Papers are legally filed to allow Grace to become Norma Jeane's legal guardian

1937

Spring   Grace becomes Norma Jeane's legal guardian

26 Jun   Norma Jeane leaves the orphanage and lives with Grace and her new husband

Nov   Norma Jeane goes to live with Ida Martin, a distant relative in Compton, LA

1938

Aug   Norma Jeane goes to live with Anna Lower, Grace's aunt

1941

Dec   Norma Jeane begins dating Jim Dougherty

1942

19 Jun   Norma Jeane marries Jim Dougherty and the newlyweds move into an apartment

1943

Spring   Jim and Norma Jeane move back to his parents' home, to look after it while they are away

Autumn   The young couple move into their own apartment again

Jim Dougherty is called up and joins the Merchant Marines – he is sent first as an instructor to Catalina Island

1944

Spring   Jim is posted to a ship in the South Pacific

Apr   Norma Jeane returns to her mother-in-law's home and starts work at Radio Plane Munitions Factory in Burbank, California

1945

26 Jun   At Radio Plane, Norma Jeane is photographed by David Conover for a feature in *Yank* magazine

2 Aug   Norma Jeane is taken on by the Blue Book Agency

1946

26 Apr   First appearance of Norma Jeane on the cover of a national magazine, *Family Circle*

Jun   Norma Jeane dyes her brunette hair blonde

Jul   Harry Lipton of National Concert Artists Corporation becomes Norma Jeane's agent

16 Jul   Norma Jeane has her first interview with Ben Lyon at 20th Century Fox studios

19 Jul   At a screen test for 20th Century Fox, Norma Jeane comes over very well

29 Jul   First mention of Norma Jeane (as Jean Norman) in a Hollywood gossip column

26 Aug   The aspiring actress signs her first studio contract, with 20th Century Fox, and changes her name to Marilyn Monroe

Sept   While in Las Vegas to obtain her divorce, Norma Jeane spends time

in Las Vegas General Hospital, first with an acute mouth infection after her wisdom teeth are removed, and then with measles

13 Sept   Norma Jeane is granted a divorce from Jim Dougherty in Las Vegas, Nevada

1947

Summer   Filming of *Dangerous Years*, with Marilyn's first speaking role

Although Marilyn's first movie role is in *Scudda Hoo, Scudda Hay*, most of her part is later cut

26 Jul   Marilyn is told that her contract with 20th Century Fox is not to be renewed

25 Aug   Marilyn's contract with 20th Century Fox runs out

4 Dec   Marilyn signs a management contract with Lucille Ryman and John Carroll

7 Dec   Release of *Dangerous Years*

1948

Feb   Marilyn meets Joe Schenck at a Hollywood party

20 Feb   Marilyn is crowned Miss California Artichoke Queen

14 Apr   *Scudda Hoo, Scudda Hay* is released

9 Mar   Marilyn signs a six-month contract with Columbia

Vocal coach Fred Karger works with Marilyn on her songs for *Ladies of the Chorus*, but her devotion to him is not reciprocated

Apr   Marilyn meets Natasha Lytess, head drama coach at Columbia, who later becomes her personal drama coach for some years

Filming of *Ladies of the Chorus*

9 Sept   Marilyn's contract with Columbia is not renewed

22 Oct	Release of *Ladies of the Chorus*
31 Dec	Marilyn meets agent Johnny Hyde from the William Morris Agency at Sam Spiegel's New Year party

1949

Feb	Marilyn films a part in *Love Happy*, and is mentioned in Louella Parsons' gossip column
27 May	Marilyn poses nude for the famous calendar photograph by Tom Kelley, which is published anonymously
24 Jul	Earl Wilson first interviews Marilyn
15 Aug	Start of shooting on *A Ticket to Tomahawk*
	Johnny Hyde becomes Marilyn's agent
	Marilyn films a small uncredited part in *Right Cross*
Oct	MGM give Marilyn a contract for a role in *The Asphalt Jungle*
10 Oct	*Life* magazine shows pictures of Marilyn in a feature about Hollywood's aspiring stars

1950

5 Jan	Marilyn begins shooting *The Fireball*
8 Apr	Release of *Love Happy*
27 Mar	Marilyn lands the part of a starlet in *All About Eve*
19 May	Release of *A Ticket to Tomahawk*
23 May	World premiere of *The Asphalt Jungle* at Grauman's Egyptian Theater
14 Oct	Release of *All About Eve*
9 Nov	Release of *The Fireball*
15 Nov	Release of *Right Cross*
10 Dec	Marilyn signs a new contract with 20th Century Fox
18 Dec	Johnny Hyde dies of a heart attack
Dec	Marilyn has minor plastic surgery, possibly to remove a small lump from her nose
Dec	Marilyn appears in *As Young As You Feel* for Fox
Dec	Arthur Miller and Marilyn meet for the first time on the set of *As Young As You Feel* on set at 20th Century Fox

1951

Mar	After catching the attention of Spyros Skouras, president of Fox, Marilyn secures the renewal of her contract
29 Mar	Marilyn is a presenter at the 1951 Academy Awards ceremony

18 Apr	Marilyn starts shooting *Love Nest* for Fox
11 May	The six-month contract with Fox is converted to a seven-year contract
	Release of *Hometown Story*
	Films a part in *Let's Make It Legal* for Fox
2 Aug	Release of *As Young As You Feel*
21 Aug	Fox agrees to loan Marilyn to RKO, to appear in *Clash by Night*
8 Sept	The first full-length feature on Marilyn appears in *Collier's* magazine
Autumn	Marilyn tries to contact C. Stanley Gifford, the man she believed was her father, but he refuses to see her
	Marilyn enrols to study acting with coach Michael Chekov
	Filming of *Clash by Night*
	Filming of *Don't Bother to Knock*
10 Oct	Release of *Love Nest*
23 Oct	Marilyn appears on the cover of *Look* magazine for the first time
6 Nov	Release of *Let's Make It Legal*
15 Nov	*Quick* magazine has a feature on Marilyn as its cover story, designating her 'The New Jean Harlow'
Dec	*Focus* magazine has a cover story on Marilyn, comparing her favourably with Lana Turner, Betty Grable and Rita Hayworth

1952

26 Feb	Marilyn begins filming *Monkey Business*
13 Mar	After the press discover Marilyn's nude calendar picture, she admits publicly that she is the model
15 Mar	Joe DiMaggio and Marilyn meet for the first time
7 Apr	Marilyn features on her first *Life* magazine cover
28 Apr	Marilyn's appendix is removed at the Cedars of Lebanon hospital
3 May	Studio publicity about Marilyn had presented her as an orphan, but after it is discovered that her mother is still alive, she releases a short statement to the press
1 Jun	Marilyn learns she has the part of Lorelei in *Gentlemen Prefer Blondes*
Jun	Start of filming of *Niagara*
18 Jun	Release of *Clash By Night*
12 Jul	General release of *We're Not Married*
18 Jul	Release of *Don't Bother to Knock*
Aug	New York premiere of *Don't Bother to Knock*
31 Aug	Marilyn's first live radio show is

	broadcast, in which she reads a role in a one-act play
1 Sept	The U.S. Army photographs Marilyn to use in a recruitment drive, but the pictures are withdrawn after the photographer shoots from a balcony, revealing too much of the Monroe cleavage
2 Sept	At the Miss America beauty pageant, Marilyn is a Grand Marshal
5 Sept	General release of *Monkey Business*
16 Oct	Release of *O Henry's Full House*
26 Oct	Marilyn is heard on ventriloquist Edgar Bergen's radio show
17 Nov	Filming begins on *Gentlemen Prefer Blondes*
22 Nov	An article titled 'The Truth about Me' appears in *The American Weekly*, with Marilyn's name as the by-line

1953

Jan	The famous nude picture of Marilyn is republished as 'Miss Golden Dreams' on the January page of a new calendar
21 Jan	*Niagara* is released
9 Feb	Gladys Baker is transferred to Rockhaven Sanatorium at Marilyn's expense
6 Mar	Filming on *Gentlemen Prefer Blondes* is completed
9 Mar	Scandal follows Marilyn's appearance at the *Photoplay* magazine awards in the tissue-thin gold lamé gown from *Gentlemen Prefer Blondes*
Mar	*Photoplay* features an article by Jim Dougherty, 'Marilyn Monroe Was My Wife'
Apr	Start of filming on *How to Marry a Millionaire*
May	Marilyn is featured on the cover of *Cosmopolitan* magazine
26 Jun	Marilyn and Jane Russell both leave their prints outside Grauman's Chinese Theater
15 Jul	Release of *Gentlemen Prefer Blondes*
Aug	Filming of *River of No Return* in Canada
20 Aug	During filming, Marilyn slips and damages her leg
Aug	Official premiere of *Gentlemen Prefer Blondes* at Grauman's Chinese Theater
13 Sept	Marilyn's made her first television appearance on *The Jack Benny Show*
Oct	Marilyn signs a recording contract with RCA
10 Oct	Marilyn accompanies Joe

	DiMaggio to visit his family in San Francisco
4 Nov	Premiere of *How to Marry a Millionaire* in Los Angeles
Dec	The famous nude calendar shot appears in the first issue of *Playboy* magazine, as the first Sweetheart of the Month, and a clothed Marilyn also appears on the cover
15 Dec	Marilyn fails to report on the first day of rehearsals of *The Girl in Pink Tights*

1954

4 Jan	Fox suspends Marilyn for failing to appear for filming
14 Jan	Marilyn marries baseball player Joe DiMaggio at San Francisco City Hall
2 Feb	The couple arrive in Tokyo for their honeymoon
16 Feb	During their honeymoon, Marilyn takes time to entertain the troops in Korea
5 Mar	Marilyn arrives back in Los Angeles
14 Mar	Marilyn is voted Best New Actress of 1953 by *Photoplay* magazine
31 Mar	Charles Feldman at Famous Artists Agency officially becomes Marilyn's agent
14 Apr	After the lifting of her suspension, Marilyn returns to the studio
30 Apr	Release of *River of No Return*
28 May	Starts filming *There's No Business Like Show Business*
7 Jul	A representative of the armed forces presents Marilyn with a trophy and plaque for morale-building activities
10 Aug	Filming begins on *The Seven Year Itch*
9 Sept	Marilyn arrives in New York for location filming on *The Seven Year Itch*
10 Sept	Milton Greene photographs Marilyn as a ballerina
16 Sept	The famous skirt-blowing sequence for *The Seven Year Itch* is filmed on the streets of New York
5 Oct	Marilyn and Joe DiMaggio officially separate
27 Oct	A divorce from DiMaggio is granted, but not finalized for one year
4 Nov	Shooting finishes on *The Seven Year Itch*
5 Nov	Joe DiMaggio and Frank Sinatra carry out the 'Wrong Door' raid, attempting to find Marilyn
6 Nov	Marilyn is honoured at a Hollywood party at Romanoff's

7 Nov	Marilyn enters the Cedars of Lebanon Hospital to undergo surgery for endometriosis
Dec	Leaving Hollywood, Marilyn heads for New York
16 Dec	Release of *There's No Business Like Show Business*
31 Dec	Marilyn Monroe Productions is officially formed

1955

7 Jan	Milton Greene and Marilyn hold a Press conference to announce the creation of Marilyn Monroe Productions
10 Jan	Marilyn returns briefly to Hollywood to film one scene of additional dialogue for *The Seven Year Itch*
15 Jan	Fox suspends Marilyn again
Feb	Marilyn begins to study under Lee Strasberg, founder of the Actors Studio in New York
9 Mar	At the premiere of *East of Eden*, Marilyn acts as an usherette in aid of the Actors Studio
30 Mar	At the opening of the Ringling Brothers Barnum & Bailey Circus, Marilyn appears riding a pink elephant in aid of the New York Arthritis & Rheumatism Foundation
8 Apr	Edward R. Murrow interviews Marilyn live on *Person to Person*
Summer	Marilyn briefly dates Marlon Brando, and when they split up they remain friends
1 Jun	World premiere of *The Seven Year Itch*
26 Jul	Breaking her agency contract with Famous Artists, Marilyn signs with MCA
29 Sept	Marilyn attends the opening night of Arthur Miller's play, *A View from the Bridge*, at New York's Coronet Theater
31 Oct	The divorce from Joe DiMaggio is finalized
31 Dec	Marilyn signs a new four-picture, seven-year contract with Fox

1956

4 Jan	Twentieth Century Fox announce that they and Marilyn have come to terms, and that she will be returning to Hollywood
9 Feb	At a Press conference in New York, Laurence Olivier announces their joint project, *The Prince and the Showgirl*
17 Feb	Marilyn performs at the Actors Studio, New York
23 Feb	Norma Jeane legally changes her name to Marilyn Monroe

25 Feb	Marilyn returns to Hollywood after her one-year exile in New York
3 Mar	Filming begins on *Bus Stop*
12 Apr	Suffering from bronchitis, Marilyn spends four days in St Vincent Hospital, Los Angeles
14 May	*Time* magazine features Marilyn on the cover for the first and only time in her lifetime
11 Jun	A divorce is granted to playwright Arthur Miller
29 Jun	Marilyn marries Miller in a civil ceremony
1 Jul	Marilyn and Miller have a Jewish wedding ceremony
14 Jul	The Millers fly to London
7 Aug	*The Prince and the Showgirl* starts filming in England
31 Aug	Release of *Bus Stop*
Sept	Marilyn becomes pregnant, but loses the baby within a few weeks
29 Oct	Marilyn is presented to Queen Elizabeth II at the Royal Command Performance of *The Battle of the River Plate* in London
17 Nov	Filming completed on *The Prince and the Showgirl*
20 Nov	The Millers return to America
18 Dec	Marilyn does a radio show broadcast from the Waldorf-Astoria

1957

18 Feb	Miller is indicted by a federal grand jury on two counts of contempt of Congress
27 Feb	Frank Sinatra testifies at an investigation into the 'Wrong Door' raid carried out by Joe DiMaggio in 1954
1 Mar	At a first hearing, Miller pleads not guilty
11 Apr	A statement is released, accusing Greene of mismanaging Marilyn Monroe Productions
14 May	After being called to Washington, Arthur Miller is put on trial for contempt of Congress; Marilyn accompanies him but stays out of sight
13 Jun	Premiere of *The Prince and the Showgirl*
1 Aug	Marilyn is rushed to Doctors Hospital, New York, with severe abdominal pain, which turns out to be an ectopic pregnancy that has to be terminated
10 Aug	Marilyn leaves hospital under a barrage of Press attention

1958

28 Jan	Marilyn attends the annual March of Dimes fashion show at the Waldorf-Astoria, New York

4 Apr	After prevaricating, Marilyn signs the contract for *Some Like It Hot*
7 Jul	Marilyn returns to Hollywood to prepare for filming
4 Aug	Filming begins on *Some Like It Hot*
Oct	Marilyn becomes pregnant again
6 Nov	Filming on *Some Like It Hot* is completed
16 Dec	Marilyn miscarries the baby, and is taken to Polyclinic Hospital in New York

1959

29 Mar	Premiere of *Some Like It Hot* at Loew's Capitol Theater on Broadway
Jun	Marilyn receives the David Di Donatello statuette from Italy for her performance in *The Prince and the Showgirl*
23 Jun	Corrective gynaecological surgery is carried out on Marilyn at the Lennox Hill Hospital, New York, to try to cure her chronic endometriosis
18 Sept	The Russian premier, Nikita Khrushchev, meets Marilyn at a luncheon in his honour at the 20th Century Fox studios in Hollywood
14 Oct	Although Marilyn is due to begin rehearsing in New York for *The Billionaire* – later released as *Let's Make Love* – she fails to show
9 Nov	Marilyn officially begins work on *Let's Make Love*

1960

25 Jan	The first part of one of Marilyn's musical numbers in *Let's Make Love* is finally filmed
8 Mar	Marilyn receives a Golden Globe award for Best Actress in a Comedy, for *Some Like It Hot*
	Yves Montand and Marilyn have a brief affair during the filming of *Let's Make Love*
Jun	Psychoanalyst Ralph Greenson begins seeing Marilyn on a daily basis
18 Jul	Filming begins on *The Misfits*
27 Aug	Marilyn is admitted to Westside Hospital in Los Angeles suffering from exhaustion
5 Sept	Marilyn returns to Nevada to finish location filming on *The Misfits*
8 Sept	Release of *Let's Make Love*
4 Nov	Shooting finishes on *The Misfits*
Nov	Yves Montand sees Marilyn briefly in New York, before returning to his wife in France

11 Nov	Arthur Miller and Marilyn officially separate
16 Nov	Clark Gable dies of a heart attack

1961

20 Jan	A divorce from Arthur Miller is granted in Juarez, Mexico
31 Jan	Premiere of *The Misfits*
7 Feb	Marilyn enters the Payne-Whitney Clinic in New York under the name Faye Miller
11 Feb	After three days, Joe DiMaggio arranges for Marilyn to be transferred to the Neurological Institute at Columbia-Presbyterian Hospital
5 Mar	Marilyn leaves the Columbia-Presbyterian Hospital
Mar	Margaret Parton interviews Marilyn for the *Ladies' Home Journal*, but the interview is never published as it is deemed 'too sympathetic' by the editor
May	Again Marilyn enters the Cedars of Lebanon Hospital for a minor operation
Summer	Frank Sinatra and Marilyn have a brief affair
28 June	Marilyn enters Polyclinic Hospital in New York to have her gall bladder removed
11 Jul	Marilyn leaves hospital
8 Aug	Finally giving up on New York, Marilyn returns to Hollywood
Oct	Robert Kennedy and Marilyn begin an affair, after meeting at Peter Lawford's beach house
19 Nov	Marilyn attends a dinner at Peter Lawford's beach house, President John Kennedy is also present

1962

Feb	Marilyn buys a new home in Brentwood, California
21 Feb	With her housekeeper, Marilyn flies to Mexico to buy furniture and artefacts for her new home
2 Mar	Marilyn returns from Mexico
5 Mar	At the Golden Globe Awards, Marilyn is presented with a statuette as the World's Favorite Female Star
10 Apr	Marilyn attends costume and makeup tests for *Something's Got To Give*
23 Apr	Filming begins on *Something's Got To Give*
19 May	Marilyn sings 'Happy Birthday' at a gala birthday party for President John Kennedy at Madison Square Garden
28 May	During filming, Marilyn is photographed swimming nude in a pool

1 Jun	Marilyn's last public appearance	20 Jul	Marilyn enters the Cedars of Lebanon Hospital for an operation to cure her endometriosis	8 Aug	Marilyn's funeral, at Westwood Memorial Park, in Los Angeles, California
8 Jun	Marilyn is fired from *Something's Got To Give* for persistent absenteeism	28 Jul	Marilyn spends the weekend at Cal-Neva Lodge		

1 Jun — Marilyn's last public appearance

8 Jun — Marilyn is fired from *Something's Got To Give* for persistent absenteeism

23 Jun — First *Vogue* photo session with Bert Stein

28 Jun — Negotiations with Fox begin about resuming work on *Something's Got To Give*

29 Jun — Start of a three-day photo session, with George Barris shooting Marilyn for *Cosmopolitan*

4 Jul — Richard Meryman begins an extensive interview with Marilyn, which turns out to be her last

12 Jul — Marilyn meets the studio chiefs at Fox

20 Jul — Marilyn enters the Cedars of Lebanon Hospital for an operation to cure her endometriosis

28 Jul — Marilyn spends the weekend at Cal-Neva Lodge

1 Aug — Fox revises Marilyn's contract, offering double her previous salary and agreeing to restart shooting on *Something's Got To Give*

3 Aug — Marilyn appears on the cover of *Life* magazine for the last time before her death

4 Aug — Dr Ralph Greenson spends six hours with Marilyn

5 Aug — Police are called after Marilyn is found dead in her Brentwood home

8 Aug — Marilyn's funeral, at Westwood Memorial Park, in Los Angeles, California

1995

1 Jun — A 32¢ commemorative postage stamp featuring Marilyn is issued in the US Legends of Hollywood series

Oct — Marilyn is voted UK's *Empire* magazine's Sexiest Female Movie Star of All Time

1997

Oct — Marilyn is listed No.8 in the UK's *Empire* magazine's The Top 100 Movie Stars of All Time

1998

Autumn — Marilyn is voted *Playboy* magazine's Sexiest Female Star of the Twentieth Century

1999

Oct — At a Christie's auction of Marilyn memorabilia, the gown in which Marilyn sang 'Happy Birthday' to John Kennedy is sold for over $1 million

Dec — *Playboy* magazine names Marilyn as No.1 Sex Star of the Twentieth Century

PICTURE ACKNOWLEDGEMENTS

All images courtesy of Corbis except the following:

Getty Images: 6, 28, 72, 73, 193, 194, 201, 202

Associated Newspapers Archive: 11, 13, 152, 153, 154, 156, 157, 158, 160, 162